MODERN ROLE MODELS

Angelina Jolie

Lydia Bjornlund

Mason Crest Publishers

Produced by OTTN Publishing in association with
21st Century Publishing and Communications, Inc.

MASON CREST PUBLISHERS INC.
370 Reed Road
Broomall, Pennsylvania 19008
(866) MCP-BOOK (toll free)
www.masoncrest.com

Printed in the United States of America.

First Printing

9 8 7 6 5 4 3 2 1

Library of Congress Cataloging-in-Publication Data

Bjornlund, Lydia D.
    Angelina Jolie / Lydia Bjornlund.
       p. cm. — (Modern role models)
    ISBN-13: 978-1-4222-0504-4 (hardcover) — ISBN-13: 978-1-4222-0791-8 (pbk.)
    1. Jolie, Angelina, 1975– —Juvenile literature. 2. Motion picture actors and
actresses—United States—Biography—Juvenile literature. I. Title.
    PN2287.J583B56 2008
    791.4302'8092—dc22
    [B]   2008020404

Publisher's note:
All quotations in this book come from original sources, and contain the spelling
and grammatical inconsistencies of the original text.

CROSS-CURRENTS

*In the ebb and flow of the currents of life we are each influenced
by many people, places, and events that we directly experience
or have learned about. Throughout the chapters of this book you
will come across **CROSS-CURRENTS** reference boxes. These
boxes direct you to a **CROSS-CURRENTS** section in the back
of the book that contains fascinating and informative sidebars
and related pictures. Go on. ▸▸*

CONTENTS

Actress Angelina Jolie, in her role as goodwill ambassador for the United Nations High Commissioner for Refugees (UNHCR). Since August of 2001 Jolie has traveled around the world to publicize the plight of, and advocate for, people who have fled their countries to escape political persecution, armed conflict, or genocide.

Ambassador to the World

ON AUGUST 27, 2001, THE OFFICE OF THE UNITED
Nations High Commissioner for Refugees (UNHCR)
named Angelina Jolie a "goodwill ambassador."
Goodwill ambassadors are well-known people who
use their fame to bring attention to
the work of the United Nations. In a
press conference, the actress explained
why she was interested in working to
publicize the problems of **refugees**:

CROSS-CURRENTS
To learn about the UN office
that Angelina represents as a
goodwill ambassador, read
"The United Nations High
Commissioner for Refugees."
Go to page 46. ▶▶

**❝We cannot close ourselves off to
information and ignore the fact that millions of
people are out there suffering. I honestly want to**

help. I don't believe I feel differently from other people. I think we all want justice and equality, a chance for a life with meaning. All of us would like to believe that if we were in a bad situation some- one would help us. **99**

Angelina had first become aware of several worldwide **humanitarian** crises while filming *Tomb Raider* in Cambodia. Deeply affected by her experience there, she sought out more information. She became active in a number of humanitarian efforts.

⇒ A COMPASSIONATE HEART ⇐

Since 2001, Angelina has used her superstar status to generate media coverage about the plight of refugees and the conditions under which they live. She has traveled widely to remote parts of the world. As a goodwill ambassador, she has visited refugee camps and receiving centers in more than 20 countries in Africa, Asia, and South America. She has also visited people seeking **asylum** at detention centers in the United States. She has met thousands of men, women, and children forced to flee their homes. She later talked about the impact that the daily struggle of refugees to stay alive has had on her life:

CROSS-CURRENTS

For more information about the UN's use of celebrities to promote its programs, check out "United Nations Goodwill Ambassadors." Go to page 47. ▶▶

"You go to these places and you realize what life's really about and what people are really going through. These people are my heroes. **99**

Ruud Lubbers, the UN High Commissioner for Refugees, said of Angelina's work:

"Since her appointment as a Goodwill Ambassador, Angelina has more than fulfilled my expectations. She has proven to be a close partner and a genuine colleague in our efforts to find solutions for the world's refugees. Above all, she has helped to make the tragedy of refugees real to everyone who will listen. Angelina's interest in helping refugees,

her personal generosity, and her truly compassion-
ate spirit are an inspiration to us all. **"**

Angelina has been a generous giver to the cause for which she
works so hard. She pays her own expenses while on missions. She
has donated millions of dollars to field operations in Africa, Asia,
the Middle East, the Balkans, and South and Central America and
is often the first private donor to respond to UNHCR appeals for emer-
gencies and forgotten refugee crises across the globe. She contributed
$1 million to help Afghan refugees seeking asylum in Pakistan and
Iran and another $1 million to the humanitarian effort assisting
millions of people affected by the crisis in Sudan's Darfur region.

**In August 2001, Angelina Jolie spent a week visiting refugee
camps in Pakistan. Here she clowns around with Afghan
children at the Jalozai camp near Peshawar, the capital of
Pakistan's North West Frontier Province. The children's
families had fled violence in northern Afghanistan. On
August 27, 2001, the day after Angelina left Pakistan, she
was named a goodwill ambassador for the UNHCR.**

Angelina with a young mother during one of her trips to Africa on behalf of the UNHCR. Of the people she met who were swept up in the continent's terrible conflicts, Angelina said, "[They] have seen so much, they've felt so much pain—lost more than anyone could bear, and yet they contain joy of life and appreciation for small things we often forget."

She also has put her acting talents to use for the cause. In 2005, she filmed an MTV special entitled "The Diary of Angelina Jolie and Dr. Jeffrey Sachs in Africa," which told of her experiences in several remote villages in Kenya. For World Refugee Day in 2006, Angelina appeared in a 30-second **public service announcement** (PSA) urging the world not to forget refugees. The PSA was broadcast around the world.

⇒ STOPPING THE CYCLE ⇐

Angelina has discussed the need for long-term solutions and justice. In 2004, Angelina visited the poverty-stricken country of Chad, where thousands of refugees from Sudan's Darfur region sought sanctuary. It was estimated that 1,000 people were dying each week from systematic attacks on their villages in Darfur. When she returned three years later, the violence had escalated. In a 2007 article published in the *Washington Post*, Angelina wrote of the cycle of violence and the need for bringing those responsible to justice.

> **In my five years with UNHCR, I have visited more than 20 refugee camps in Sierra Leone, Congo, Kosovo and elsewhere. I have met families uprooted by conflict and lobbied governments to help them. Years later, I have found myself at the same camps, hearing the same stories and seeing the same lack of clean water, medicine, security and hope. It has become clear to me that there will be no enduring peace without justice. History shows that there will be another Darfur, another exodus, in a vicious cycle of bloodshed and retribution. But an international court finally exists. It will be as strong as the support we give it. This might be the moment we stop the cycle of violence and end our tolerance for crimes against humanity.**

More recently, Angelina has visited Afghanistan and Iraq, where more than 2 million people—more than half of whom are under the age of 12—have been displaced by war. In a follow-up story she wrote for the *Economist*, she stressed the importance of helping refugees:

> **What happens in Iraq and how Iraq settles in the years to come is going to affect the entire Middle East. And a big part of what it's going to affect, how it settles, is how these people are returned and settled into their homes and their community and brought back together and whether they can live together and what their communities look like.**

As a UN goodwill ambassador and as a Hollywood icon, Angelina has continued to work to tell others about the plight of the world's refugees and to find them the help they so desperately need.

Angelina rebelled during her early teen years. She dyed her hair purple and began dressing in dark clothes. At age 14, she stopped going to school. With her live-in boyfriend, she spent much of her time partying at clubs. Beneath this wild lifestyle, however, Angelina was struggling with emotional pain and depression.

Wild Child

ANGELINA JOLIE VOIGHT WAS BORN ON JUNE 4, 1975, in Los Angeles. She seemed destined to become an actress. Her father, Jon Voight, had already achieved fame as an actor. Her mother, Marcheline Bertrand, was a model and actress. Leading actress Jacqueline Bisset and actor/**director** Maximilian Schell were named her godparents.

CROSS-CURRENTS

If you're interested in finding out more about Angelina Jolie's father's life and career, read "Jon Voight." Go to page 48. ▶▶

Angelina's parents separated when she was a baby. Her mother abandoned her dream of acting and moved with Angelina and her older brother James to Palisades, New York. Like other little girls, Angelina loved to wear plastic high heels and sparkly clothes. She loved being the center of attention and would flounce around to make the adults laugh. In a CNN interview with Paula Zahn, her father Jon remembers her as a child:

❝She was dramatic when she was a young girl, and she was always dressing up and designing little things, skits for her friends and so on. I saw her—you know, I thought maybe this gal would become an actress.❞

In fact, Jon played a key role in Angelina's acting **debut**. When Angelina was seven, she had a bit part as his daughter in *Lookin' to Get Out*, a movie that Jon not only starred in but also cowrote. Marcheline also had a small role. Angelina saw little of her father, however, and blamed him for leaving her mother.

➤ BACK TO HOLLYWOOD ➤

When Angelina was 11, she and her family moved back to Los Angeles. Angelina entered the Lee Strasberg Theatre Institute, an acting school that her mother had attended. Over the next two years, she appeared in several stage productions, but Angelina was not sure acting was for her. She toyed with the idea of becoming a funeral director instead.

Angelina had some unusual interests. She collected—and continues to collect—knives. She favored snakes and iguanas over dogs and cats.

Angelina did not fit in with the Beverly Hills crowd. Other students ridiculed her big lips and distinctive features. She could not afford the finest clothes like the other kids, and her secondhand clothes never seemed to fit her too-thin body quite right. The fact that she wore glasses and braces added to her insecurity.

➤ A DARK SIDE ➤

By the time she was a teen, Angelina had begun to show a dark side. She dressed in black and dyed her hair purple. She struggled with depression and filled her school notebooks with drawings of knives and daggers. She did not like to be touched, even by her mother. One day, she began to cut herself. She later explained in a 2005 interview with CNN:

❝For some reason, the ritual of having cut myself and feeling the pain, maybe feeling alive, feeling some kind of release, it was somehow therapeutic to me.❞

From her childhood years, Angelina preferred snakes to dogs and cats. "I suppose I like the thing that everybody doesn't," she revealed. "I think [snakes are] magnificent creatures. . . . [Handling snakes is] something that people are afraid of. . . . I believe in conquering our fears immediately or getting over anything you hesitate with."

By 14, Angelina was living hard and fast. She stopped attending school. Her boyfriend moved in with her in her mother's home, and they started going to clubs. She still has a faint scar from the time her live-in boyfriend complied with Angelina's request to draw a knife blade along her jawline. In a *Rolling Stone* interview, she remembered their relationship:

❝Looking back, I think I was probably not good for him. He was somebody that I wanted to help me break out and I would get frustrated when he

couldn't help me. Which was when the knives came in—he'd be asked to cut me or I'd cut him. **"**

⇒ ACTING AGAIN ⇐

Angelina soon chose a more constructive path. At 16, she ended her relationship with her boyfriend and moved into an apartment near her mother. She returned to high school and to acting. In 1991, she made her stage debut in a play called *Room Service*. She also starred in five films that her brother made while he was a student at the University of Southern California's film school, and appeared in music videos for Meat Loaf, Lenny Kravitz, the Lemonheads, and the Rolling Stones.

In 1993, she got her first break, starring in *Cyborg 2* as a sexy human-like robot built to blow up the enemies of her creators. Two years later, she starred in *Hackers*. On the set, Angelina met and fell in love with Jonny Lee Miller, her costar in the movie.

Angelina was not yet famous, but she began to catch the attention of the press and public with her open manner and her unconventional ways. In 1996 Angelina and Jonny were married in a highly unusual ceremony. Rather than the usual white gown, the bride wore black rubber pants and a white shirt with Jonny's name scrawled on the back in her own blood. She also revealed that she had gotten several tattoos—an unusual step for Hollywood beauties. The media buzzed with stories about her obsession with death, her collection of knives, and her other unusual interests.

CROSS-CURRENTS

Today, Angelina Jolie has more than a dozen tattoos. For more information about them, read "Angelina's Tattoos." Go to page 49. ▶▶

⇒ ANGELINA WINS GOLD ⇐

Some people wondered whether Angelina would be able to live down her wild reputation and be taken seriously as an actress. Her talent would soon prove their concern misplaced.

In 1997, Angelina accepted a role as Cornelia Wallace, opposite Gary Sinise in the made-for-TV **biopic** *George Wallace*. John Frankenheimer, the movie's director, told *People* magazine that Angelina was someone to watch:

"The world is full of beautiful girls, but they're not Angelina Jolie. She's fun, honest, intelligent, gorgeous and divinely talented. **"**

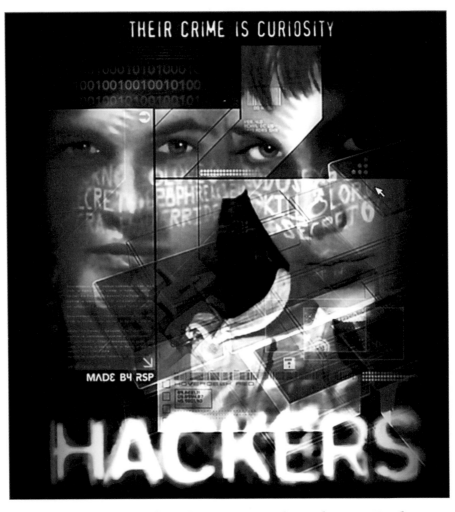

THEIR CRIME IS CURIOSITY

MADE BY RSP

HACKERS

A publicity poster for the 1995 motion picture *Hackers*, starring Angelina Jolie and Jonny Lee Miller as young computer geeks caught up in the schemes of a nefarious computer-security expert. During filming, Angelina fell in love with her costar, and she and Miller were married in 1996.

Frankenheimer was right about Angelina's talent. In 1998, Angelina won a Golden Globe and was nominated for an Emmy for her work in *George Wallace.* This was just the first sign that her star was on the rise.

By the late 1990s, Angelina Jolie had begun to attract a considerable amount of attention in show-business circles—and not simply because of her stunning beauty, unorthodox behavior, and remarkable candor in discussing her own life. Film directors, producers, and critics started to recognize Angelina's talents as an actress.

Angelina, Interrupted

IN 1998, ANGELINA ACCEPTED THE STARRING ROLE in *Gia*, an HBO movie based on the true story of a heroin-addicted supermodel who dies of AIDS. She used techniques of **method acting** and stayed in character between scenes. She did not talk to Jonny during the filming because she "was" Gia Carangi— a lesbian woman battling her addiction.

Gia left Angelina feeling drained, both physically and emotionally. In many ways, the character reminded Angelina of her own wild past, including experiments with drugs. She and Jonny soon split under the pressure, and Angelina announced that she was giving up acting for good. She later explained in an interview with *Rolling Stone*:

> **"**I felt like I'd given everything I had and I couldn't imagine what else was in me.**"**

Angelina fled Los Angeles for New York and enrolled in New York University to study filmmaking. Living in this big city in which she knew no one, she became depressed and lonely. She contemplated suicide but worried that others—especially her mother—would blame themselves. So she tried to hire a hit man to kill her. He wisely counseled her to wait a month to reconsider. Sure enough, a month later, she was feeling better.

AND THE WINNER IS . . .

Part of Angelina's healing came from success. For her portrayal of Gia Carangi, Angelina won a second Golden Globe and a Screen Actors Guild Award, and she was nominated for an Emmy Award. She later said that this was the first time she felt as though people understood her. In a 2001 interview with *Rolling Stone*, she recalled her experience at the Golden Globe award ceremony:

> **I felt like somebody who had crashed some party, and suddenly it became easier for me to work. I thought my life was completely meaningless and that I would never be able to communicate anything and that there was nobody who understood . . . and then I realized I wasn't alone. Somehow life changed.**

But Angelina showed no sign of becoming the typical Hollywood leading lady. After winning the Golden Globe, she enthusiastically jumped into the pool at the Beverly Hilton Hotel—still wearing her designer gown. She later told *Playboy* that her response was in keeping with the spirit of the evening:

> **What's funny to me is that everyone wasn't jumping into the pool. It's one of those events, and the people in the room are supposed to be free and wild, but everyone is so tame and careful.**

MORE MOVIES

Success brought a new level of professional respect and recognition. Angelina was soon appearing on talk shows and in magazines, and people were intrigued by her willingness to talk openly about her unusual opinions and behaviors.

Angelina holds up the Golden Globe trophy she received for Best Actress in a Miniseries or Motion Picture Made for Television, at the 56th Annual Golden Globe Awards, held January 24, 1999, in Beverly Hills, California. Angelina was recognized for her portrayal of a drug-addicted lesbian supermodel in *Gia*.

By now, the roles were coming fast and furious for Angelina. She took a part in a gangster movie called *Hell's Kitchen* and then in a drama with an **ensemble cast**, *Playing by Heart*. Again, her acting received rave reviews by critics. She won an award for "Best Breakthrough Performance by an Actress" from the National Board of Review of Motion Pictures for her part in *Playing by Heart*.

In 1999, she accepted a part as a rookie police officer searching for a serial killer in *The Bone Collector*, starring alongside Denzel Washington. The movie grossed $151 million worldwide, but the critics liked neither the movie nor Angelina's performance. However, Philip Noyce, *The Bone Collector*'s director, was impressed by Angelina's commitment to acting. He said in an interview with *Time* magazine:

> "She's not burned out with the joy of performing. She's in her element because she can set parameters

A poster for 1999's *The Bone Collector*, which starred Denzel Washington and Angelina Jolie as homicide detectives trying to catch a vicious serial killer. The film did reasonably well at the box office, but most movie critics found fault with the plot—and with the performances of the two lead actors.

for a character, whereas I suspect she doesn't know her own boundaries emotionally and physically. I suspect she's happiest when she's not being Angelina Jolie. **"**

⇒ *GIRL, INTERRUPTED* ⇐

Angelina's big break occurred in *Girl, Interrupted*, a story about young women in a psychiatric hospital. The movie was based on a best-selling book by Susanna Kaysen. Angelina brought her tough acting skills to the part of Lisa, an inmate diagnosed as being a **sociopath**. James Mangold, the movie's director, admitted that Angelina was not always easy to work with. He told *Time* magazine in a 2000 article:

"Angie is rebellious, volatile and really smart. Playing this role put her in the mode of questioning authority. But if someone delivers the goods like she did, then I'm happy to struggle with the personality. **"**

Girl, Interrupted did not make a lot of money at the box office, and it received mixed reviews from critics. Susanna Kaysen was unhappy with the way the film turned out. However, Kaysen did say that Angelina's performance was the most true-to-life portrayal in the movie.

Girl, Interrupted was supposed to be a comeback vehicle for Winona Ryder, who played Kaysen in the film, but Angelina stole the show. She won her third Golden Globe award and, more importantly, she won the Academy Award for Best Supporting Actress for her part in the film. Academy Awards, also known as Oscars, are the most coveted trophies in Hollywood. Earning this award cemented Angelina's place as one of the best young actresses in the business.

However, during the Academy Awards ceremony in March 2000, another controversy ensued. When she accepted her award, Angelina gave her brother James a long kiss, adding, "I'm so in love with my brother right now." The tabloids went crazy. They showed pictures of the kiss and said that Angelina and her brother were "too close." Although she seemed to relish her bad girl image, Angelina was hurt that people would think that James meant anything more to her than a beloved brother should. She later said in an interview with *Vogue*:

Angelina, with costars Clea DuVall (left) and Angela Bettis (center), in a scene from *Girl, Interrupted*. The 1999 film was intended to show off the talents of its executive producer, actress Winona Ryder, but Angelina stole the show. For her role as Lisa Rowe, a former drug addict diagnosed as a sociopath, Angelina won a Golden Globe and an Academy Award.

"To me, it was just amazing that people didn't understand. Saying I'm 'in love' with him is just an expression. It's just the way I was talking. What I meant was, in this moment, with all this [stuff] going on, all that matters to me is that guy sitting right there who has stood by me and is so [very] happy for me."

➤ PUSHING THE ENVELOPE ⭐

On May 5, 2000, Angelina married Billy Bob Thornton, an award-winning actor whom she had met the previous year on the set of the movie *Pushing Tin*. Billy Bob had already been married four times and was almost 20 years older than Angelina, but Angelina believed she had found a soul mate. Angelina and Billy Bob wore jeans for their wedding. It was held in a Las Vegas chapel and cost $189. She had Billy Bob's name tattooed on her arm. Instead of wedding rings, Angelina and Billy Bob each wore a vial of the other's blood around their necks.

The couple soon became known for their wild antics. They told the press how much in love they were from the moment they met and shared personal stories about their exciting love life. Although they were not the typical happy couple, Angelina and Billy Bob seemed well matched. More and more people became captivated by Angelina's rebellious nature, and many magazines and newspapers began to run stories about her activities.

CROSS-CURRENTS

If you want to know more about Billy Bob Thornton's life and career, check out "Billy Bob Thornton." Go to page 50. ▶▶

In the summer of 2000, Angelina starred with Nicholas Cage in the action film *Gone in 60 Seconds*. The movie was a big hit, earning more than $240 million at the box office. But bigger things were ahead for Angelina.

➤ LARA CROFT ⭐

In 2000, director Simon West picked Angelina to star in *Lara Croft: Tomb Raider*. The movie, which was released in 2001, is based on a popular video game and centers on a female action character. The role was far different from the dark, complex characters that had earned Angelina so much praise, but West later said that he could not imagine anyone else as Lara:

> **She's totally right for the role. It's like finding Sean Connery in 1962 for James Bond. I now can't see how I'd have done the film without her.**

For her part, Angelina was excited about the physical challenges of playing the part of Lara Croft. She trained for ten weeks prior to the film to gain weight and build muscle. She did much of her own

Angelina Jolie as the title character of *Lara Croft: Tomb Raider*. Her role in the 2001 film was quite a departure for Angelina. Instead of the dark, complicated characters she had portrayed previously, Angelina took on the role of action-hero. Audiences responded favorably, and *Tomb Raider* topped $275 million in box-office receipts.

stunt work and had to learn martial arts and sword fighting. She also had to learn how to speak with a British accent.

The departure from brooding characters was a welcome relief for Angelina. In an interview for *Tiscali Film & TV*, she later explained her decision to take the role:

> **People told me I should be doing things considered to be more serious. I have drowned in being deep and complicated and dark. It's sometimes hard in life to be free so I thought I want to go on this adventure. This is the first time I've happened to do something mainstream and have some fun with it.**

Tomb Raider earned more than $275 million and reached a wider audience than any of Angelina's previous films. It was one of the most successful films of the year, and firmly established Angelina as a movie star with international appeal. It also changed her life in several other unpredictable ways. It provided an opportunity for Angelina to forge a stronger relationship with her father, Jon Voight, who played the role of Lara Croft's father in the movie. Jon told the *New Zealand Herald* what it was like to work with his daughter:

> **As a father, spending time with your children is the greatest thing, so to get to work with Angelina was very satisfying. It was also quite worrying because Angelina insisted on doing the majority of her stunts. I'd be on the sidelines with the stunt coordinator saying, 'You're pushing her too hard,' or pulling her aside and telling her she was taking too many risks. But she wouldn't listen. She's too independent, too headstrong.**

Angelina later said that working together had helped father and daughter talk together in ways they had not previously. Angelina also learned from Lara Croft's can-do spirit. She told *Rolling Stone* magazine:

> **If Lara Croft's got a problem, she gets up and fixes it. If she's frustrated she breaks something. That's what life can be.**

In 2003 Angelina visited the Democratic Republic of Congo along with John Prendergast, senior adviser to the humanitarian organization International Crisis Group. Aided by two photographers, Angelina and Prendergast produced a Web journal, *Ripples of Genocide: Journey Through Eastern Congo*. It publicized the plight of people caught up in the incredibly brutal war in the Congo.

Going Global

WHEN ANGELINA JOLIE WAS WORKING ON *TOMB* *Raider* in Cambodia, she witnessed the natural beauty and culture of this country. At the same time, however, she saw extreme poverty. Cambodia is a small country in Southeast Asia that was torn by civil war throughout the 1970s and 1980s. Its people remain among the poorest in the world.

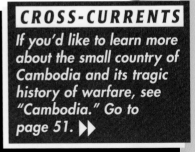

CROSS-CURRENTS

If you'd like to learn more about the small country of Cambodia and its tragic history of warfare, see "Cambodia." Go to page 51. ▶▶

Because of the long-running civil war, millions of landmines are still buried under Cambodian soil. Every year, hundreds of people, mostly civilians, are injured or killed when they accidentally set off mines. Angelina was shocked to see children who had lost limbs because of landmines. The experience changed her life, and she has often spoken about her observations in Cambodia. In a 2001 interview, she said:

> **"I don't want to get into the heaviness of it here, but I discovered things about what's happening in the world. Like my eyes started to open. . . . To know that there are hospitals where kids are still being affected by stepping on landmines every day was horrifying and so sad. You never hear about that. To discover that kind of stuff was to really understand people in the rest of the world."**

After completing the filming for *Lara Croft: Tomb Raider*, Angelina began visiting refugee camps. In 2001, she was appointed as a goodwill ambassador for the UNHCR and began to spend more and more time on humanitarian efforts. She has repeatedly told the press that by doing this important work, she had finally found her life's meaning.

⇒ NEW PRIORITIES ⇐

Angelina's life changed in another way also. In the spring of 2002, she adopted a seven-month-old baby boy from an orphanage in Cambodia. Angelina took to motherhood almost immediately, saying that her son Maddox—whom she called "Mad"—provided her life with meaning. In an interview published in *Vogue*, she explained how adopting Maddox had changed her outlook on life:

> **"I'm committed to the future now. I'm committed to life. I think definitely before my son, I was a little nihilistic. But once I adopted Mad I knew I was never going to be intentionally self-destructive again."**

However, Angelina's new priorities put a strain on her marriage to Billy Bob Thornton. In July 2002, just two months after their second wedding anniversary, Angelina filed for a divorce. As usual, Angelina spoke openly in interviews, telling about the breakup and how she felt about it. In an interview with *US Weekly*, she said:

> **"I'm angry. I'm sad. It's a very difficult and sad time. Sometimes, you don't see things coming, even though they are happening. It was a real deep con-nection, a deep marriage, so it's not that simple to**

Angelina with her son Maddox, a Cambodian orphan she adopted in 2002. The child, Angelina told an interviewer, dramatically changed her outlook. "I'm committed to the future now," she said. "I'm committed to life. . . . Once I adopted Mad I knew I was never going to be intentionally self-destructive again."

say this or that one thing caused the problems. It's clear to me that our priorities shifted overnight. He's focused on his music and career. I'm focused on my baby. It comes down to what's important to you. **"**

In response to the couple's breakup, Angelina's father, Jon Voight, told the television program *Access Hollywood* that he thought Angelina had serious mental problems. Angelina's mother came to her defense, saying that there was nothing wrong with her mental health—a diagnosis with which many of her coworkers agreed. Angelina herself responded to her father's comments by legally removing Voight from her name and refusing to see or talk to him.

⇒ PUBLICIZING HER MISSIONS ⇐

Meanwhile, Angelina was traveling feverishly on behalf of UNHCR. During her travels, she kept a journal. In 2003, her writings about early missions to Africa, Cambodia, Pakistan, and Ecuador were published as a book titled *Notes from My Travels*. All of the money from the sale of the book goes to charity. The book has received rave reviews by readers, who say they are touched by her candid descriptions of the people she meets.

At the same time, she appeared in a movie that reflected her real-life interest in the refugee crisis. *Beyond Borders*, which was about aid workers in Africa, was not as well received as Angelina's book had been. The *Los Angeles Times* review of the 2003 film was typical:

CROSS-CURRENTS

To find out what Angelina was thinking as she set out to help refugees, read "Notes from My Travels." Go to page 52. ▶▶

> **Making the picture seems to have changed star Angelina Jolie's life, turning her into a United Nations goodwill ambassador, and care was taken to shoot the film in a series of far-flung countries. But the hard truth is that the line between being deadly earnest and unintentionally silly is thinner than these people think, and 'Beyond Borders' turns out to be an unreal film about a real situation, unavoidably cartoonish.**

Angelina had greater success when she revisited the role of Lara Croft in 2003's *The Cradle of Life*. The **sequel** did almost as well as the original, earning more than $160 million. Angelina said she enjoyed the experience—for which she was paid $12 million.

Angelina brought Maddox with her on many of her travels. As a sign of devotion to her son, she went to Thailand to have a Buddhist prayer of protection tattooed in Cambodian Sanskrit on her left shoulder blade. Although she sometimes has to cover up her tattoos with makeup for her movies, this and her other tattoos are clearly visible on most other occasions.

In 2004, Angelina had another busy year. She starred in the thriller *Taking Lives*, and appeared in the film *Sky Captain and the World of Tomorrow*. Angelina also lent her voice to the character of Lola, an angelfish, in the animated movie *Shark Tale*; other celebrities who participated in the film included Will Smith, Renée Zellweger, and Robert De Niro. But her biggest movie of the year was *Alexander*, a film directed by Oliver Stone about the ancient conqueror Alexander the Great. Although it was heavily

In director Oliver Stone's *Alexander* (2004), Angelina played Queen Olympias, the mother of the fourth century B.C. Macedonian general Alexander the Great, who was played by Colin Farrell (right). Val Kilmer (center) costarred as King Philip II. The big-budget biopic wasn't a huge hit with American audiences, but it did well internationally.

promoted, American audiences did not like the film. *Alexander* did better internationally, however, and ended up making a respectable $165 million at the box office.

➤ A NEW LOVE ⬅

In 2004, Angelina filmed *Mr. & Mrs. Smith*, an action-comedy that told the story of contract assassins who are married. Both spouses have been living secret lives for years without the other knowing about their work. Angelina received $20 million for the part, becoming the third woman (after Julia Roberts and Cameron Diaz) to command such a high salary for a film role. The money was well spent. *Mr. & Mrs. Smith* became one of the biggest hits of 2005, earning more than $186 million in the United States alone.

Almost immediately, rumors began to spread about the relationship between Angelina and costar Brad Pitt. While Angelina was a well-known and talented actress, Brad was an international superstar. Brad had wed *Friends* star Jennifer Aniston in a million-dollar ceremony in 2000. Most people thought they had a solid marriage . . . until *Mr. & Mrs. Smith*. Hollywood gossips believed that Angelina and Brad's on-screen chemistry was fueled by an off-camera love affair.

CROSS-CURRENTS

Brad Pitt is respected both for his acting talent and for his humanitarian work. To learn more, read "Brad Pitt." Go to page 53. ▶▶

Angelina denied having an affair with Brad Pitt. She said that she would never date a married man. She knew firsthand the hurt that an affair with a married man causes because her father had cheated on her mother. She added that she would never respect a man who cheated on his wife.

Still, as Brad and Jennifer's separation and divorce became public, Angelina and Brad started to be seen together. Newspapers and magazines ran pictures of the couple and started to refer to them as "Brangelina." In a 2005 interview in *Vogue*, Angelina explained that she and Brad had been friends long before they fell in love.

❝Brad was a huge surprise to me. I, like most people, had a very distant impression of him from the media. I think we were both the last two people who were looking for a relationship. I certainly wasn't. I was quite content to be a single mom with

**Angelina and Brad Pitt, her costar in the action-comedy hit
Mr. & Mrs. Smith (2005), sign autographs for fans. During
filming of the movie, tabloid newspapers linked Angelina
romantically with her married costar, a charge she denied.
The two were seen together increasingly often after Brad's
2005 divorce from actress Jennifer Aniston.**

Mad. And I didn't know much about exactly where
Brad was in his personal life. But it was clear he was
with his best friend, someone he loves and respects.
And so we were both living, I suppose, very full lives. 〞

In 2005, Brad joined Angelina in Ethiopia to adopt her second
child, an AIDS orphan named Zahara. Angelina says that the children
contributed to cementing her relationship with Brad. In the *Vogue*
interview, she told of Maddox's role in bringing them together:

"It's a big thing to bring together a child and a father. It had never crossed my mind that Mad was going to need a father—certainly not that it would be this man I just met. Until, of course, I got to know Brad and realized that he is naturally just a wonderful father. And we left a lot of it to Mad, and he took his time and then . . . just out of the blue called him Dad."

⧉ LOBBYING FOR CHANGE ⧉

In addition to traveling on behalf of UNHCR, Angelina has traveled to Washington, D.C., many times to meet with members of Congress to

At the annual meeting of the World Economic Forum in Davos, Switzerland, Angelina Jolie attends a session devoted to the UN's Millennium Development Goals (MDGs), January 17, 2005. The eight MDGs include eradicating extreme poverty and hunger; achieving universal primary education; improving maternal health; and ensuring environmental sustainability.

lobby on behalf of refugee children. Among her concerns is passage of the Unaccompanied Child Protection Act, which would provide legal counsel and assistance to children who travel to the United States without their parents. Angelina argues that these children cannot figure out how to apply for asylum. In a UNHCR statement, she said:

> **Over 6,000 children arrive alone in the United States every year. Some are fleeing persecution, many are fleeing abuse. Some are trafficked to work as prostitutes or in sweatshops. Many are eligible for asylum or other humanitarian status in the United States, but U.S. laws do not give them the legal assistance they need to apply. The court process is so complex that children cannot be expected to be able to apply for asylum or other legal status by themselves.**

Some congressional leaders have stopped the bill's passage because they say it will cost too much. In 2005, Angelina responded by giving $500,000 to the National Center for Refugee and Immigrant Children, which provides free legal advice to children seeking asylum. She explains her decision:

> **It is unethical to not listen to these children. Because without legal representation we are sending children to court to represent themselves in a language that most of them don't understand. And expecting them to recall accounts so frightening and humiliating, they wouldn't want to tell anyone, let alone a room full of strangers.**

At the Jabel Sharoon camp in Pakistan, Angelina Jolie listens to a woman made homeless by the October 5, 2005, earthquake centered in the Kashmir region along the India-Pakistan border. The powerful quake, which measured 7.6 on the Richter scale, killed more than 70,000 people and left millions homeless.

A Life
Worth Living

AS ANGELINA CONTINUED TO WORK ON BEHALF of refugees around the world, she began bringing Brad Pitt along with her. In 2005, the couple spent Thanksgiving weekend in Pakistan, where a massive earthquake had killed 73,000 people and destroyed entire villages. More than 3 million people were left homeless. Angelina and Brad brought emergency supplies and renewed hope.

Angelina loved helping others. In a 2005 interview with CNN, she said:

> **"My role as goodwill ambassador has made my work as a film star relatively dull. I can't find anything that interests me enough to go back to work."**

Yet Angelina did continue to work in movies. She costarred with Matt Damon in *The Good Shepherd*, a movie about the early days of the Central Intelligence Agency. Matt Damon played a spy; Angelina was his long-suffering wife. In a *Vogue* story about Angelina, director Robert De Niro said he was nervous about casting Angelina because he was not sure she would be "frumpy" enough:

> **The way the character is written, she kind of gets frumpy as she gets older. I had this preconception in my head . . . that she would become this sort of, not quite dowdy housewife, but someone who's settled into and accepted her fate. Angelina did that but in her own way, and I was very, very happy with it. Her instincts are terrific.**

Critics and some members of the public preferred Angelina as Lara Croft. The *New York Times* review said that the part did not suit Angelina:

> **It is not a good fit. A force of nature, Ms. Jolie reads more believably when she's running through the jungle in boots and a bikini, as she does in the 'Tomb Raider' flicks, than when standing on the sidelines in a domestic nightmare.**

SHILOH

Late in 2005, Brangelina fever reached new heights with the announcement that Angelina was pregnant. To avoid the media frenzy, Brad and Angelina decided to have their baby in Namibia, a small African country that Angelina had visited during the 2002 filming of *Beyond Borders*. Namibia has an HIV infection rate of more than 21 percent, but Angelina explained in an interview with *Vogue* that part of their decision was based on the relatively good health of the country:

> **We aren't completely insane. We looked for places that were not rife with malaria and dengue fever, and Namibia is good for that because it's so dry.**

CROSS-CURRENTS

Few people know much about Namibia, a small country in southern Africa. To learn more, read "Namibia." Go to page 54. ▶▶

Angelina and Brad flew to Namibia on April 3, 2006, with Maddox and Zahara. They found a luxury resort in an isolated location and rented out all rooms for ten weeks. On May 27, Angelina gave birth to a little girl. The couple named her Shiloh Nouvel Jolie-Pitt. Shiloh means "the peaceful one" in Hebrew.

In order to prevent the paparazzi from hounding them for photographs of their baby daughter Shiloh Nouvel, Angelina Jolie and Brad Pitt arranged to sell the first photos of the newborn themselves. They donated all the money—almost $10 million—to charity. Shown here is the cover of a Croatian magazine.

Knowing that the paparazzi would hound them for a shot of the baby, Angelina and Brad decided to sell Shiloh's first photos themselves. *People* magazine paid more than $4.1 million for the North American rights to the photos, and *Hello!* magazine paid $3.5 million for the international rights. This was the most that had ever been paid for photographs. Angelina and Brad donated all of the money to charity.

⋙ CHARITABLE GIVING ⋘

By now, Angelina and Brad were becoming known for their generous giving. In 2006, they founded the Jolie-Pitt Foundation and donated

Angelina Jolie and Brad Pitt move sacks of grain for distribution to victims of the 2005 earthquake in Pakistan. The two have become known for their generosity and their devotion to a variety of humanitarian causes, from aiding refugees and orphans in Africa to helping rebuild sections of hurricane-devastated New Orleans.

$1 million to Doctors Without Borders and Global Action for Children. In a statement, Jennifer Delaney, U.S. director for Global Action for Children, said:

> **" Angelina Jolie and Brad Pitt not only care, but more important, are taking concrete action to address the fact that there will be 20 million children orphaned by AIDS by 2010, and millions more orphaned by tuberculosis, malaria and conflict or whose parents are sick and dying. "**

Angelina and Brad also have given $1 million to three relief organizations that help refugees in Chad and Darfur. Many of the couple's charity choices result from very personal interests. Following the birth of their first child in Namibia, they gave $300,000 to Namibia's hospitals for maternity supplies and equipment. The pair also has pledged $5 million to set up a wildlife sanctuary in Cambodia, the native country of their oldest child Maddox. In 2007, they bought a house in New Orleans and committed funds and their energy to helping to rebuild parts of the city destroyed by Hurricane Katrina.

⇛ ANGELINA AND FAMILY LIFE ⇚

In January 2007, Marcheline Bertrand, Angelina Jolie's mother, died after a long battle with cancer. Angelina and her brother James Haven had always been close to their mother. In a December 2007 interview with *Backstage*, Angelina spoke of her mother's love and support:

> **" I used to work with my mom. She was the most amazing support for an actor. She used to write letters to my characters. For *Girl, Interrupted*, she bought me the hand puppet that I ended up using. If I'd do a sexy role, she'd buy me perfume. She always read the script, made a bunch of notes, and wrote these letters. She was a great person to talk to about things, and she loved the process so much. So now I suppose I try to hear her voice in my head. "**

Angelina, James, and Brad were with Marcheline at the hospital when she died. Angelina had always been thin, and she lost weight after her mother's death. In interviews, Angelina admitted that she was finding it difficult to eat a healthy diet.

The death of Angelina's mother renewed public attention on her estranged relationship with her father. Angelina explained to the media that she is not angry with her father, but that she believes it is unhealthy for her to talk to him.

CROSS-CURRENTS

For more details about Maddox, Zahara, Shiloh, and Pax Thien, read the short article "Angelina's Children." Go to page 54. ▶▶

Brad had adopted Maddox and Zahara, and in March 2007, the couple announced another adoption—this time a three-year-old orphan named Pax from Vietnam.

⇒ DIRECTORIAL DEBUT ⇐

In 2007, Angelina directed her first movie, *A Place in Time*. This experimental **documentary** sought to capture both the diversity of life around the globe and the commonality of the human spirit by filming in many places around the world at the same moment. In an interview with *The Japan Times*, Angelina explained her reasons for making the documentary:

> **"**Not everyone gets the chance to see how other people in other nations live. TV doesn't really show that, because it won't get high ratings . . . and the news is about very, very short segments, usually focusing on a trouble spot. Many of the people I'm interested in live in troubled areas, but the major trouble for most people in the world—and most of the world is the developing world—is poverty. Getting enough to eat . . . and so many other daily problems, things that we (in the modern world) take for granted.**"**

On the heels of *A Place in Time*, Angelina starred in the movie *A Mighty Heart*. In this **docudrama,** she played the wife of Daniel Pearl, a reporter for the *Wall Street Journal* who had been kidnapped and murdered while on assignment in Pakistan. Angelina received rave reviews for her performance. She was nominated for several awards, including a Golden Globe and a Screen Actors Guild Award.

Director Michael Winterbottom instructs a cameraman during a scene from *A Mighty Heart*. In the 2007 film, Angelina Jolie (left) portrayed Mariane Pearl, the wife of *Wall Street Journal* reporter Daniel Pearl, who was abducted and murdered in 2002 by Islamic extremists linked to the terrorist group al-Qaeda. Angelina's performance earned her several award nominations.

⇒ ANGELINA TODAY ⇐

Angelina Jolie is one of the most-recognized women in the world today. According to a global online survey conducted by the marketing firm ACNielsen, out of a random list of celebrities, Angelina Jolie and Brad Pitt were voted the best to endorse almost every category, from casual clothing to eveningwear. Angelina is routinely included on top-ten lists of beautiful women. In 2006, *People* magazine named her the "Most Beautiful Woman in the World." In February 2007, she was voted the greatest sex symbol of all time in the British Channel 4 television show *The 100 Greatest Sex Symbols*. Her lips—once ridiculed— are reportedly the most requested by people undergoing lip surgery.

Angelina has become renowned as much for her good works as for her good looks. In February 2008, *Forbes* magazine named Brad Pitt and Angelina Jolie the most influential Hollywood couple. The same year, she headlined *People* magazine's "Beauty Inside & Out" with Brad. The feature story highlighted her humanitarian work with refugees, AIDS orphans, and the **genocide** in Darfur.

Angelina also talks openly of the balance between work and family. She and Brad take turns being home with their four young children. In 2008, news broke that Angelina was pregnant with twins. The twins, Knox Leon and Vivienne Marcheline Jolie-Pitt, were born in France on July 12, 2008.

At a press conference during the annual meeting of the Clinton Global Initiative in New York, Angelina announces the creation of a program she cofounded with economist Gene B. Sperling, September 26, 2007. The Education Partnership for Children of Conflict, launched with $148 million in pledged donations, seeks to provide schooling for children in war-torn regions.

⋙ INTO THE FUTURE ⋘

No one who knew Angelina Jolie as an adolescent could have known that she would make such a huge impact in the world. The lonely, troubled teenager seemed to be headed toward a life of parties and drugs. But this former wild child has truly found something to be wild about. She has thrown her energy into helping others.

Countries and organizations around the globe have praised Angelina's work on behalf of others. She has been awarded many honors, including the United Nations Correspondents Association's first Citizen of the World Award, the Global Humanitarian Action Award from the United Nations Association of the USA and the Business Council for the United Nations, and the Humanitarian Award from the Church World Service Immigration and Refugee Program. In 2005, Angelina became an honorary citizen of Cambodia for her tireless efforts to call attention to landmines.

In a 2008 interview with *Parade* magazine, Angelina gave advice for those who want to get involved:

> **❝I think the first step is to try to navigate your way through [all the information available] and see where your heart goes. I do think it has to be personal. It has to be strong for it to last and grow, and then it will be a pleasure to work hard to do it. ❞**

Jane Goodall, a famous scientist who dedicated her life to studying chimpanzees in Africa, agrees. On the back cover of *Notes from My Travels*, she writes:

> **❝Angelina is living proof of the power we all have—every one of us—to make a difference.❞**

It seems that there is nothing that Angelina Jolie cannot do. She is a stunning beauty, a supremely talented actress, a committed activist, and a loving mother. Regardless of the role she is playing, Angelina continues to turn heads.

The United Nations High Commissioner for Refugees

The Office of the United Nations High Commissioner for Refugees (UNHCR) is an organization that protects millions of refugees around the world. Its focus is on providing emergency necessities such as food, water, shelter, and medical assistance to people fleeing their homes because of war and persecution. When possible, UNHCR helps refugees safely return to their homes. For the millions of people for whom returning home is not an option, UNHCR helps with local integration or resettlement to a third country. In addition, UNHCR promotes the legal protection of refugees and sustainable solutions through an extensive body of international law and treaties and by working with governments and other organizations on subjects ranging from promoting asylum systems to refugee advocacy.

Sacks of grain provided by the United Nations High Commissioner for Refugees sit in a field in Dadaab, Kenya, 2006. The grain was to be distributed to refugees fleeing conflict in the neighboring country of Somalia.

UNHCR was formed by the United Nations General Assembly on December 14, 1950, and has helped an estimated 50 million refugees restart their lives. The agency is mandated to lead and coordinate international action to protect refugees and resolve refugee problems

6,500 people in 122 countries around the world, making it the largest international humanitarian organization of its kind. I currently provides support for an estimated 32.9 million people around the world.

United Nations Goodwill Ambassadors

The United Nations (UN) enlists celebrity advocates as goodwill ambassadors, who use their fame to uphold the ideals of the United Nations and its agencies. The UN first began to use celebrity ambassadors in the 1950s, when Broadway and movie star Danny Kaye became an ambassador to promote children's rights. His tireless efforts over the following years created a model for other stars and other causes. Today, hundreds of international stars—from award-winning actors to sports heroes—donate their time and talents to help spread the UN's message.

The current set of celebrity advocates for the United Nations is led by a group of distinguished individuals who are known as "Messengers of Peace." Personally recruited by the UN secretary-general, the Messengers of Peace must have a good reputation, a proven interest in humanitarian issues, and global appeal. The Messengers of Peace work hard on a volunteer basis to focus attention on the work of the UN. Today's Messengers of Peace include American actors Michael Douglas and George Clooney, Brazilian author Paulo Coelho, Japanese violinist Midori Goto, and Princess Haya Bint al Hussein of Jordan.

Most UN goodwill ambassadors are recruited independently by various UN agencies. There are 13 UN agencies, and each has different groups of celebrities who contribute varying amounts of time and effort. The UN attempts to reach a global audience through its choice of ambassadors. Many of the most important representatives—such as Miss Universe Mpule Kwelagobe, who was recently appointed Goodwill Ambassador to Botswana for the UN Population Fund—may be unknown in some parts of the world.

UNICEF, the UN children's fund, currently has five goodwill ambassadors who represent the agency almost full time. The UN Development Programme uses Brazilian footballer Ronaldo to highlight the plight of the poor. Geri Halliwell, a former Spice Girl, has been a goodwill ambassador for the UN Population Fund, promoting safe sex to teenage girls in the Philippines and elsewhere. Nicole Kidman joined the ranks of goodwill ambassadors in 2006, working with the UN Development Fund for Women (UNIFEM) on gender concerns such as ending violence against women.

In addition to Angelina Jolie, the United Nations High Commissioner for Refugees (UNHCR) currently lists six other celebrities as goodwill ambassadors. They include Italian designer Giorgio Armani, French singer Julien Clerc, Egyptian actor Adel Imam, American singer Barbara Hendricks, Greek musician George Dalaras and Uruguayan actor Osvaldo Laport.

(Go back to page 6.) ◀◀

Jon Voight

Angelina Jolie's father, Jonathan Vincent Voight, has had a long career as a leading man and a character actor, playing a wide range of parts. He first gained critical acclaim in 1969's *Midnight Cowboy,* in which he played a naïve hustler from Texas who moves to New York City. Although Jon was a relative unknown, the part earned him an Academy Award nomination. In 1988, Jon won several awards for his role as a paraplegic Vietnam War veteran in *Coming Home*, including the Academy Award for Best Actor.

Jon married model/actress Marcheline Bertrand in 1971. This—his second marriage—lasted just five years; they separated in 1976 and divorced in 1978. Jon has always had a strained relationship with their children, James Haven and Angelina Jolie. By some accounts, he rarely saw them when they were little, and Angelina has said she was hurt by her father's cheating on her mother.

Actor Jon Voight, Angelina Jolie's father, has appeared in dozens of motion pictures. He won an Academy Award for his portrayal of a wheelchair-bound Vietnam War veteran in 1978's Coming Home. *Voight also shared acting credits with his daughter in the 2001 action-thriller* Lara Croft: Tomb Raider.

The relationship between father and daughter seemed to be on the mend when the two worked on the first *Tomb Raider* movie, but fell apart when Jon questioned Angelina's mental stability after her breakup with Billy Bob Thornton. The two did not speak with each other for years. Jon has said that he loves his children and has expressed sorrow that he has never met his grandchildren. (Go back to page 11.) ◀◀

Angelina's Tattoos

Angelina Jolie has more than a dozen tattoos. On her wrist she wears the letter "H," which she got while dating Timothy Hutton; she says the tattoo is in tribute to her brother, James Haven. She also has a discreet "M" on the palm of her hand in memory of her mother. After adopting Maddox, she had a Cambodian prayer tattooed on her left shoulder. She has added to her upper arm the map coordinates of where each of her children was born. The coordinates were tattooed where she had once had "Billy Bob," but that tattoo was removed by laser treatment after her divorce.

Angelina's tattoos give a glimpse into her loves and her feelings. Across the top of her back reads "know your rights." She also has marked on her body a Tennessee Williams line: "A prayer for the wild at heart, kept in cages" and "Quod me nutrit me destruit," a Latin phrase that translates to "What nourishes me also destroys me."

Other tattoos include a black cross—which she had tattooed to her groin area the day before she married Jonny Lee Miller—a dragon, and two Native American symbols. One of her most recent tattoos is of a large crouching tiger winding across the center of her lower back.

(Go back to page 14.) ◀◀

A tattoo artist inks Angelina's lower back with an image of a crouching tiger, Bangkok, Thailand, 2004. Angelina has more than a dozen tattoos. Some commemorate loved ones, including her mother, her brother, and her children. Others incorporate ideas or quotations she

Billy Bob Thornton

Billy Bob Thornton was born in Hot Springs, Arkansas, on August 4, 1955. He had bit parts on several sitcoms and small roles in several other films, including *Indecent Proposal*, *On Deadly Ground*, and *Bound by Honor*. It was with his own independent film, *Sling Blade* (1996), that he gained international acclaim. He wrote, directed, and starred in this film about a mentally handicapped man. Billy Bob won the Academy Award for Best Adapted Screenplay, a Writers Guild of America Award, and an Edgar Award for the screenplay and was nominated for an Academy Award for Best Actor.

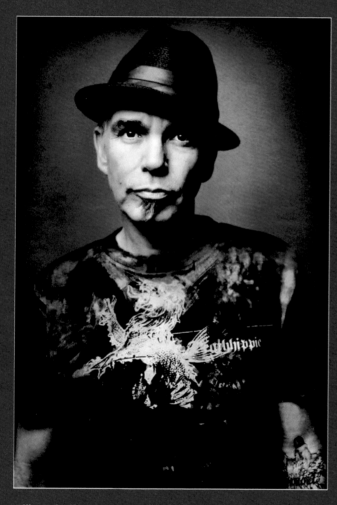

Billy Bob Thornton, Angelina Jolie's second husband, burst into the spotlight with Sling Blade, *a 1996 film he wrote, directed, and starred in. Angelina and Billy Bob met in 1999 during filming of* Pushing Tin. *They were married the following year and divorced in 2002.*

After the success of *Sling Blade*, Billy Bob's acting career took off. He took starring roles in *Primary Colors*, *Armageddon*, and *Monster's Ball*, and played Santa Claus in 2003's *Bad Santa*, a **black comedy** that did well at the box office and established Billy Bob as a leading comic actor. He followed up the success of *Bad Santa* with leading roles in *The Astronaut Farmer* and *Mr. Woodcock*, a comedy in which Billy Bob plays a sadistic gym teacher.

Billy Bob has indicated that he has obsessive-compulsive disorder and several unusual phobias. He has been married five times, most recently to Angelina Jolie. The pair was thought to be well suited because of their eccentricities, but they broke up after just a few years of marriage. (Go back to page 23.) ◀◀

Cambodia

Cambodian children at a refugee camp, early 1980s. Cambodia has been devastated by decades of fighting; the murderous regime of the Khmer Rouge, which ruled the country from 1975 to 1979; high rates of disease; and the lingering problem of landmines, which maim and kill hundreds of Cambodians every year.

Cambodia, a country in southeastern Asia, has a rich cultural history. The country suffered a series of bloody civil wars in the 1970s and 1980s, fueled in part by the conflict in neighboring Vietnam. In 1991, the United Nations was called upon to enforce a ceasefire agreement of the warring parties. As a result of the fighting, much of Cambodia's rural countryside is riddled with landmines—bombs that explode when someone steps on them.

Although today the country's population of 14 million lives in relative peace, Cambodia remains one of the world's poorest countries. Forty percent of the population lives below the official poverty rate, which is just 45 cents per person per day. Government corruption, combined with the years of fighting, has added to the country's problems. Many rural areas do not have schools or basic infrastructure. HIV and AIDS are on the rise in Cambodia, which already has the highest **infant mortality rate** in the region.

Cambodia's tropical climate gives rise to lush greenery, but it is rapidly losing its forests. Since 1970, Cambodia's primary rainforest cover fell dramatically from more than 70 percent in 1970 to just 3.1 percent in 2007. Angelina Jolie and Brad Pitt have given money to help address some of Cambodia's environmental problems. (Go back to page 27.) ◀◀

Notes from My Travels

This excerpt from Angelina Jolie's 2003 book provides insight into her thoughts as she embarked on a new chapter in her life.

In her early years as a UNHCR goodwill ambassador, Angelina wrote down her thoughts, impressions, and experiences during trips to Sierra Leone, Tanzania, Cambodia, Pakistan, and Ecuador. These writings were collected and published in 2003 by Simon & Schuster as Notes from My Travels.

"This is the beginning of my trip and my journal. I do not know who I am writing to—myself, I guess, or to everyone, whoever you are. I am not writing for the person who may read these pages, but for the people I will be writing about.

"I honestly want to help. I don't believe I am different from other people. I think we all want justice and equality. We all want a chance for a life with meaning. All of us would like to believe that if we were in a bad situation someone would help us.

"I don't know what I will accomplish on this trip. All I do know is that while I was learning more and more every day about the world and about other countries as well as my own, I realized how much I didn't know.

"I have done a lot of research and talked with many people. . . . I have read as much as I could. I discovered statistics that shocked me and stories that broke my heart. I also read many things that made me sick. I have had nightmares—not many, but they scared me."

(Go back to page 30.) ◀◀

Brad Pitt

William Bradley Pitt was born in Shawnee, Oklahoma, on December 18, 1963, and grew up in Springfield, Missouri. He moved to Beverly Hills when he was 24 years old to pursue an acting career. After small parts on several sitcoms and soap operas, Brad won a small part in the 1991 hit movie *Thelma & Louise*. After this, Brad appeared in numerous movies, including *Twelve Monkeys*, *Fight Club*, *Spy Game*, *The Mexican*, and *Ocean's Eleven*.

Brad married *Friends* actress Jennifer Aniston in 2000. Later, he and Jennifer joined Brad Grey, the head of Paramount Pictures, to found a production company called Plan B. The company produced several films, including the blockbuster hit *Charlie and the Chocolate Factory*. Amid rumors that Brad and Angelina were having an affair, Brad and Jennifer divorced in 2005.

Brad Pitt continues to be one of Hollywood's most popular leading men. In 2006, he starred in *Babel*; the following year, in *Ocean's Thirteen*, with George Clooney and Matt Damon. He has twice been named the "Sexiest Man Alive" by *People* magazine. Brad has also been an active supporter of medical research for AIDS and other diseases. He is behind Not on Our Watch, an organization that focuses global attention and resources on stopping and preventing mass atrocities.

Angelina Jolie and Brad Pitt at the 64th Annual Golden Globe Awards, held in Beverly Hills, California, January 15, 2007. The two Hollywood superstars met in 2004 on the set of the action-comedy film Mr. & Mrs. Smith.

(Go back to page 32.)

Namibia

When Brad Pitt and Angelina Jolie wanted to escape the media frenzy to have their first baby, they went to Namibia, a country in southern Africa. This large, arid country shares a border with Angola to the north, Botswana to the east, and South Africa to the south. With a population of just over 2 million, Namibia is one of the least densely populated countries in the world.

Namibia is known for its contrasting landscapes. The desolate Namib Desert is said to be the oldest desert in the world, with its high dunes and awe-inspiring sense of space. The Kaokoland Mountains run along the coast in the northwest part of the country. Inland lies the Etosha Pan (a dried-out salt lake), surrounded by grasslands and bush that support varied wildlife. The Etosha National Park & Game Reserve remains to a large extent free of human influence.

Although many people were shocked by Brad and Angelina's decision to give birth in Namibia, those who know the country understood their decision. The country has a stable government and little crime. Moreover, the private hospitals are excellent, accommodations are clean and modern, and most of the country is free of malaria. As promised, Brad and Angelina got the privacy they desired.

(Go back to page 38.) ◀◀

Angelina's Children

Angelina Jolie has six children—three of them adopted, and three with Brad Pitt. Brad has also adopted her other three children and acts as a father to them.

Angelina's first child, Maddox Chivan Jolie-Pitt, was born on August 5, 2001, as Rath Vibol in Cambodia. Maddox was adopted on March 10, 2002, when he was seven months old. Prior to the adoption, he lived in an orphanage in Battambang, Cambodia's second-largest city. Angelina adopted Maddox when she was married to Billy Bob Thornton. He has appeared regularly in the tabloid media and was named the "cutest celebrity kid" in 2006 by *America's Life and Style* magazine.

Zahara Marley Jolie-Pitt, Angelina's second child, was born on January 8, 2005, in Ethiopia. She was adopted from an Addis Ababa orphanage when she was six months old. Brad accompanied Angelina to Ethiopia to adopt Zahara. Although only Angelina's name was included on the adoption papers, she later said that she and Brad had together decided to adopt the child. Shortly after they returned to the United States, Zahara was hospitalized for an intestinal infection, dehydration, and malnutrition. Initial reports indicated that Zahara's mother had died of AIDS. When her mother was found alive, rumors followed that she wanted Jolie to give her child back. However, the Ethiopian woman denied these rumors, saying that she was glad that Zahara would be taken care of by such a famous person.

The cover story of the March 19, 2007, issue of People *magazine centered on the growing family of Brad Pitt and Angelina Jolie. Brad is holding their daughter Shiloh Nouvel, while Angelina holds their daughter Zahara Marley. The couple also adopted a three-year-old Vietnamese boy, Pax Thien, from an orphanage in 2007.*

Shiloh Nouvel Jolie-Pitt is Angelina's first biological child. Shiloh was born on May 27, 2006, by a scheduled cesarean section undertaken by Angelina's Los Angeles obstetrician and local staff at Cottage Medi-Clinic Hospital in Swakopmund, Namibia. The rights for the first pictures of baby Shiloh earned almost $10 million worldwide. Angelina and Brad donated this money to charity. Shiloh became the first infant to be included in the collection of the famous wax museum Madame Tussauds of New York.

Born on November 29, 2003, as Pham Quang Sang in Vietnam, Pax Thien Jolie-Pitt was adopted by Angelina in 2007. Pax had been found outside a hospital shortly after his birth and had lived in an orphanage since. Because the orphanage does not allow unmarried couples to adopt, Angelina adopted Pax as a single parent. Brad added his name to the adoption papers after they returned to the United States.

On July 12, 2008, Angelina gave birth to fraternal twins, Knox Leon and Vivienne Marcheline Jolie-Pitt, in Nice, France. Both of the children weigh about five pounds at birth.

(Go back to page 42.) ◀◀

1975   Angelina Jolie Voight is born on June 4 in Los Angeles, California.

1976   Angelina's parents separate; her mother moves to Palisades, New York, with Angelina and brother James Haven.

1982   Angelina has her first movie part, playing father Jon Voight's daughter in *Lookin' to Get Out*.

1986   Marcheline Bertrand moves her children back to Los Angeles; Angelina enrolls in the Lee Strasberg Theatre Institute.

1996   Angelina marries British actor Jonny Lee Miller; the couple divorces three years later.

1998   Angelina wins her first Golden Globe, for *George Wallace*.

1999   Angelina takes home an Academy Award for *Girl, Interrupted*.

2000   Angelina marries Billy Bob Thornton in a $189 ceremony in Las Vegas. While filming *Lara Croft: Tomb Raider* in Cambodia, Angelina becomes aware of that country's many problems, which she calls an eye-opening experience.

2001   Angelina is named a goodwill ambassador for the UNHCR.

2002   Angelina adopts seven-month-old Maddox in Cambodia. Following Jon Voight's comments after her divorce from Billy Bob Thornton, she cuts off all contact with her father. For many years, she refuses to speak to him or let him see her children.

2003   Angelina publishes journals of her work as goodwill ambassador as *Notes from My Travels*; she also films *Beyond Borders*.

2004   Angelina becomes just the third woman to earn $20 million for a film (*Mr. & Mrs. Smith*). While filming, Angelina meets Brad Pitt, and rumors circulate that they are having an affair.

2005   Photos surface confirming a relationship between Angelina and Brad. In July, Angelina adopts six-month-old Zahara Marley from an Ethiopian orphanage. Angelina also announces the creation of the National Center for Refugee and Immigrant Children, which she endows with $2 million.

2006   Brad Pitt legally adds his name as father for Angelina's two adopted children. Angelina, Brad, and their two adopted children travel to Namibia, where Angelina gives birth to Shiloh Nouvel Jolie-Pitt on May 27, 2006. The couple sells the rights to Shiloh's first photos and gives the money earned to charity.

2007   Angelina's mother dies after a long battle with cancer. In March, Brad and Angelina adopt three-year-old Pax Thien Jolie-Pitt in Vietnam. Angelina directs her first movie, the documentary *A Place in Time*.

2008   Angelina is nominated for several awards for her part in *A Mighty Heart*. Gives birth to twins Knox Leon and Vivienne Marcheline Jolie-Pitt on July 12, 2008, in Nice, France.

Filmography

1982	Lookin' to Get Out	2002	Life or Something Like It
1993	Cyborg 2	2003	Lara Croft Tomb Raider: The Cradle of Life
1995	Hackers		Beyond Borders
1996	Mojave Moon	2004	Taking Lives
	Love Is All There Is		Shark Tale
	Foxfire		Sky Captain and the World of Tomorrow
1997	Playing God		Alexander
	True Women (TV)	2005	Mr. & Mrs. Smith
	George Wallace (TV)	2006	The Good Shepherd
1998	Gia (TV)	2007	A Mighty Heart
	Hell's Kitchen		Beowulf
	Playing by Heart	2008	Wanted
	Pushing Tin		Kung Fu Panda
1999	The Bone Collector		Changeling
	Girl, Interrupted		
2000	Gone in 60 Seconds		
2001	Lara Croft: Tomb Raider		
	Original Sin		

Awards and Award Nominations

Acting

1998 Golden Globe Award, Best Supporting Actress for Series/Miniseries/TV Movie (*George Wallace*)

Nominated, Emmy Award, Outstanding Supporting Actress in a Miniseries or a Movie (*George Wallace*)

National Board of Review of Motion Pictures Award, Breakthrough Performance—Female (*Playing by Heart*)

1999 Golden Globe Award, Best Performance by an Actress in a Miniseries or Motion Picture Made for TV (*Gia*)

Screen Actors Guild Award, Outstanding Performance by a Female Actor in a TV Movie or Miniseries (*Gia*)

Nominated, Emmy Award, Outstanding Lead Actress in a Miniseries or a Movie (*Gia*)

2000 Academy Award, Best Actress in a Supporting Role (*Girl, Interrupted*)

Golden Globe Award, Best Performance by an Actress in a Supporting Role in a Motion Picture (*Girl, Interrupted*)

Screen Actors Guild Award, Outstanding Performance by a Female Actor in a Supporting Role (*Girl, Interrupted*)

Blockbuster Entertainment Award, Favorite Supporting Actress–Drama (*Girl, Interrupted*)

Broadcast Film Critics Association, Critics Choice Award (*Girl, Interrupted*)

Nominated, Blockbuster Entertainment Award, Favorite Supporting Actress–Drama (*The Bone Collector*)

Hollywood Film Festival, Actress of the Year

2001   Blockbuster Entertainment Award, Favorite Supporting Actress–Action (*Gone in 60 Seconds*)

Nominated, Teen Choice Award, Film–Choice Actress (*Lara Croft: Tomb Raider*)

2005   Peoples Choice Award, Favorite Female Action Movie Star

2008   Nominated, Golden Globe Award, Best Performance by an Actress in a Motion Picture–Drama (*A Mighty Heart*)

Nominated, Screen Actors Guild Award, Outstanding Performance by a Female Actor in a Leading Role (*A Mighty Heart*)

Nominated, Broadcast Film Critics Association, Critics Choice Award (*A Mighty Heart*)

Humanitarian Awards

2002   Church World Service, Immigration and Refugee Program Humanitarian Award

2003   United Nations Correspondents Association, Citizen of the World Award

2005   United Nations Association of the United States of America, Global Humanitarian Award
King Norodom Sihamoni, Cambodia, honorary citizenship

2007   International Rescue Committee, Freedom Award

Books

Jolie, Angelina. *Notes from My Travels*. New York: Simon & Schuster, 2003.

Lynette, Rachelle. *Angelina Jolie*. San Diego: Lucent Books, 2006.

McFay, Edgar. *Angelina Jolie: Angel in Disguise*. Fort Lauderdale, FL: Icon Press, 2005.

Mercer, Rhona. *Angelina Jolie*. London: John Blake Publishing, 2007.

Pearl, Mariane, and Angelina Jolie. *In Search of Hope: The Global Diaries of Mariane Pearl*. Brooklyn, NY: powerHouse Books, 2007.

Web Sites

www.angelinafans.com

Designed for fans, this Web site includes the latest photos of and information on Angelina Jolie.

www.imdb.com

The Internet Movie Database contains information and reviews of thousands of films, as well as movie industry people and news.

www.people.com

People magazine's searchable Web site includes news articles, photographs, and video clips of celebrities; Angelina Jolie is among the celebrities featured in the biographies section.

www.rollingstone.com

The Internet version of *Rolling Stone* magazine includes several interesting articles on and interviews with Angelina Jolie.

www.tiscali.co.uk

This British Internet site offers movie reviews and biographical sketches, news, and interviews with film and TV stars.

www.unhcr.org

The United Nations High Commissioner for Refugees site provides comprehensive news and information on Angelina Jolie's work around the world, including her journal entries.

www.wutheringjolie.com

This fan club site has provided information and news on Angelina Jolie since 1998.

Publisher's note:

The Web sites mentioned in this book were active at the time of publication. The publisher is not responsible for Web sites that have changed their addresses or discontinued operation since the date of publication. The publisher will review and update the Web site addresses each time the book is reprinted.

asylum—shelter and protection, including that granted by a government to someone who has fled another country because of persecution or war.

biopic—a combination of the words "biography" and "picture," used to describe a film that is based on a person's life.

black comedy—a comedy that focuses on serious issues and/or includes humor about unpleasant aspects of life.

debut—first public appearance or presentation of an actor or other performer.

director—the person who is in charge of guiding the actors in their performances and who directs the filming of a motion picture.

docudrama—a dramatized television program or movie based on actual events.

documentary—a movie or TV program presenting facts and information, especially about a political, historical, or social issue.

ensemble cast—a group of actors who have roughly equal contributions, with no one person playing the lead role.

genocide—the systematic killing of people from a national, ethnic, or religious group.

humanitarian—somebody who actively works to improve the lives of others, especially those less fortunate.

infant mortality rate—the number of deaths during the first year of life per thousand live births, this statistic is one measurement of the health of a nation or people.

method acting—a system of acting in which the actor identifies strongly with the internal motivation of the character.

public service announcement—an announcement on television or radio serving the public interest and run by the media at no charge.

refugee—somebody who seeks or takes shelter in a foreign country to avoid war or persecution.

sequel—a published book, movie, or other work that continues a story, generally by using the same characters.

sociopath—a person who displays a pervasive pattern of disregard for, and violation of, the rights of other people.

Chapter 1: Ambassador to the World

p. 5 "We cannot close ourselves off . . ." United Nations High Commissioner for Refugees Press Release, "Angelina Jolie named UNHCR Goodwill Ambassador for Refugees," www.unhcr.org, August 23, 2001.

p. 6 "You go to these places . . ." Tim Saunders, "Angelina Jolie: Helping Her Heroes," www.looktothestars.org/news/547-angelina-jolie-helping-her-heroes, February 15, 2008.

p. 6 "Since her appointment . . ." Ruud Lubbers, the UN High Commissioner for Refugees, foreword to *Notes from My Travels* (New York: Simon and Schuster, 2003), 2.

p. 9 "In my five years . . ." Angelina Jolie, "Justice for Darfur," *Washington Post* (February 28, 2007), A19.

p. 9 "What happens in Iraq . . ." Associated Press, "Angelina Jolie Visits Baghdad as U.N. Goodwill Ambassador to Highlight Plight of Refugees," StarTribune.com, www.startribune.com/entertainment/movies/15393886.html, February 6, 2008.

Chapter 2: Wild Child

p. 12 "She was dramatic . . ." CNN, "Paula Zahn Now," transcripts.cnn.com/TRANSCRIPTS/0506/09/pzn.01.html, June 9, 2005.

p. 12 "For some reason . . ." CNN, "Paula Zahn Now."

p. 13 "Looking back . . ." Chris Heath, "Blood, Sugar, Sex, Magic," *Rolling Stone*, www.rollingstone.com/news/story/5938014/blood_sugar_sex_magic, July 5, 2001.

p. 14 "The world is . . ." "Angelina Jolie," People.com, www.people.com/people/angelina_jolie/biography.

Chapter 3: Angelina, Interrupted

p. 17 "I felt like I'd . . ." Heath, "Blood, Sugar, Sex, Magic."

p. 18 "I felt like somebody who . . ." Heath, "Blood, Sugar, Sex, Magic."

p. 18 "What's funny . . ." "Angelina Jolie," People.com.

p. 20 "She's not burned out . . ." Jeffrey Ressner, "Rebel without a Pause," *Time*, www.time.com/time/magazine/article/0,9171,995905,00.html, January 24, 2000.

p. 21 "Angie is rebellious . . ." Ressner, "Rebel without a Pause."

p. 21 "I'm so in love . . ." Myrddin Gwynedd, "Best and Worst Oscar Speeches Ever," *New Zealand Herald*, February 5, 2008. http://www.nzherald.co.nz/event/story.cfm?c_id=604&objectid=10494427

p. 22 "To me, it was . . ." Jonathan Van Meter, "Angelina Jolie: Body Beautiful," *Vogue*. www.style.com/vogue/feature/032602/page2.html, April 2002.

p. 23 "She's totally right . . ." Tiscali Film & TV, "Lara Croft Live and Kicking," *tiscali.film & tv*, www.tiscali.co.uk/entertainment/film/interviews/angelina_jolie.html.

p. 25 "People told me . . ." Tiscali Film & TV, "Lara Croft Live and Kicking."

p. 25 "As a father . . ." Desmond Sampson, "Jon Voight Feels Fine in a Supporting Role," *New Zealand Herald*, www.nzherald.co.nz/sectoin/6/story.cfm?c_id=6&objectid=217837, September 19, 2001.

p. 25 "If Lara Croft's got a . . ." Heath, "Blood, Sugar, Sex, Magic."

Chapter 4: Going Global

p. 28 "I don't want to . . ." Prairie Miller, "Angelina Jolie on Filling Lara Croft's Shoes and D-Sized Cups," *NY Rock*, www.nyrock.com/interviews/2001/jolie_int.asp, June 2001.

p. 28 "I'm committed to the future . . ." Van Meter, "Angelina Jolie: Body Beautiful."

p. 28 "I'm angry . . ." Press Release, "Angelina Says She Has Split Up With Billy Bob," Cinema.com, www.cinema.com/news/item/6062/angelina-says-she-has-split-up-with-billy-bob.phtml, July 18, 2002.

p. 30 "Making the picture seems . . ." Kenneth Turan, "Movie Review: Beyond Borders," *Los Angeles Times*, www.calendarlive.com/movies/reviews/cl-et-borders24oct24,2,3041228.story?coll=cl-mreview, October 24, 2003.

p. 32 "Brad was a huge surprise . . ." Van Meter, "Angelina Jolie."

p. 34 "It's a big thing . . ." Van Meter, "Angelina Jolie."

p. 35 "Over 6,000 children . . ." Angelina Jolie, "Raising Awareness," UNHRC, www.unhcr.org/help/HELP/4399b9322.html.

p. 35 "It is unethical . . ." UN News Centre, "UN Goodwill Ambassador Jolie Launches Centre for Refugee Children in US," www.un.org/apps/news/story.asp?NewsID=13595&Cr=asylum&Cr1 March 10, 2005.

Chapter 5: A Life Worth Living

p. 37 "My role as goodwill ambassador . . ." CNN, "Paula Zahn Now."

p. 38 "The way the character . . ." Van Meter, "Angelina Jolie."

p. 38 "It is not a good . . ." Manohla Dargis, "The Good Shepherd: Company Man: Hush, Hush, Sweet Operative," *New York Times*, movies.nytimes.com/2006/12/22/movies/22shep.html, December 22, 2006.

p. 38 "We aren't completely insane . . ." Van Meter, "Angelina Jolie."

p. 41 "Angelina Jolie and Brad Pitt . . ." Press Release, "Angelina Jolie and Brad Pitt Donate $1 Million to Global Action for Children," Global Action for Children, www.globalactionforchildren.org/news/angelina_jolie_and_brad_pitt_donate_1_million_to_global_action_for_children, September 20, 2006.

p. 41 "I used to work . . ." Jenelle Riley, "Close to Her Heart," *Backstage*, www.backstage.com/bso/search/article_display.jsp?vnu_content_id=1003679575, January 2007.

p. 42 "Not everyone gets a chance . . ." George Hadley-Garcia, "Angelina Jolie: True to Her Heart," *Japan Times Online*, search.japantimes.co.jp/cgi-bin/ff20070705r1.html, July 5, 2007.

p. 45 "I think the first step . . ." "Angelina Jolie" *Parade*, www.parade.com/celebrity/articles/070530-Angelina-Jolie.html, February 17, 2008.

p. 45 "Angelina is living proof . . ." Jolie, *Notes from My Travels*, back cover.

Numbers in **bold italics** refer to captions.

Lydia Bjornlund is a freelance writer in Virginia, where she lives with her husband, Gerry Hoetmer; their children, Jake and Sophia; and their two cats. She has written eight nonfiction books for children, mostly on American history and government topics. She also has written dozens of books and training materials for adults. Ms. Bjornlund holds a master's degree in education from Harvard University and a bachelor of arts from Williams College.

PICTURE CREDITS

page

1: SIPA Press

4: Adlan Khasanov/Reuters

7: UNHCR/PRMS

8: E. Parsons/UNHCR/PRMS

10: ASP Library

13: Starstock/Photoshot Images

15: MGM/NMI

16: ASP Library

19: AP Photo

20: Universal Pictures/NMI

22: Columbia Pictures/NMI

24: Paramount Pictures/PRMS

26: Getty Images

29: X17Agency/CIC Photos

31: Warner Bros./NMI

33: Gamma Presse

34: Severin Nowacki/World Economic Forum/PRMS

36: J. Redden/UNHCR/PRMS

39: Extra/NMI

40: J. Redden/UNHCR/PRMS

43: Paramount Vantage/FPS

44: Lindsay Beyerstein/CIC Photos

46: U.S. DoD/PRMS

48: U.S. Marie Corp./PRMS

49: STR/AFP/Getty Images

50: ASP Library

51: R. Yates/UIUC

52: Tanya Makeyeva/UNHCR/PRMS

53: D'Orazio & Asso. for Bochic/PRMS

55: People Magazine/NMI

Front cover: Corbis Outline